Dear friend,

I am so glad this book has found its way to you.

Picture story books are a great tool to introduce or extend children's (and our) understanding of a topic. They can be enjoyed over and over again, each time revealing a new gem.

The intention of this book is to support you in your conversations with children in relation to the Martyrdom of the Báb. While this historical episode of the Faith can seem like a solemn tale to tell, I believe we cannot underestimate the capacity of our children to start to learn about the nature of the sacrifice the Báb made in giving His life, even at an early age.

It is therefore my sincere hope that this book can provide a valuable resource for children to develop an ever increasing understanding of the significance of this Holy Day, with your additional loving guidance.

Much love and prayers coming your way, wherever you may be.

- Helen

Remembering our dear friend Gunnar
who reminded us that all is well.

H.F & L.K.S

When The Smoke Cleared

By Helen Flynn

Illustrations by Louisa Kwan Shabani

On a morn in July,
in a town called Tabríz,
Alí witnessed what happened
to the Báb and Anís.

Like every morn,
he woke to fetch bread,
but the market was filled
with a big crowd instead.

People whispered and stared
at the bleak barrack wall.
Young Ali thought
"How I wish I was tall."

So he climbed on a roof
from where he could see...

... about **TEN THOUSAND** people

All facing two men
suspended by ropes.
"In my heart I can feel,
They carry all our hopes."

One wears a green turban,
"A Siyyid He must be.
What I would give for Him
to glance at me."

like waves on a sea.

Ali rushed down the stairs towards his heart's desire when murmur and shouting was replaced with:

"FIRE!"

Smoke filled the square.
Once more he heard

"FIRE!"

At the third round
of bullets,
the air felt dire.

When the smoke cleared,
all eyes looked around.
Anís was untied.
The Báb was not found.

Guards started searching.
"I must follow their lead!
  If I am quiet enough,
  I might meet the Siyyid."

In His cell He was peaceful.
The guards were amazed.
How could this happen
right before their gaze?!?

"His face is radiant,
His sweet voice divine,
His words are connecting
His pure heart to mine."

Then the Báb raised His head.
"Proceed with your intention."
Among the last words that
He wished to mention.

Guards lead Him back
towards the bleak barrack wall,
where hearts were deaf
toward His mighty call.

"Please let me through!
Move out of my way!"
When the crowd heard these words,
the Báb had to say:

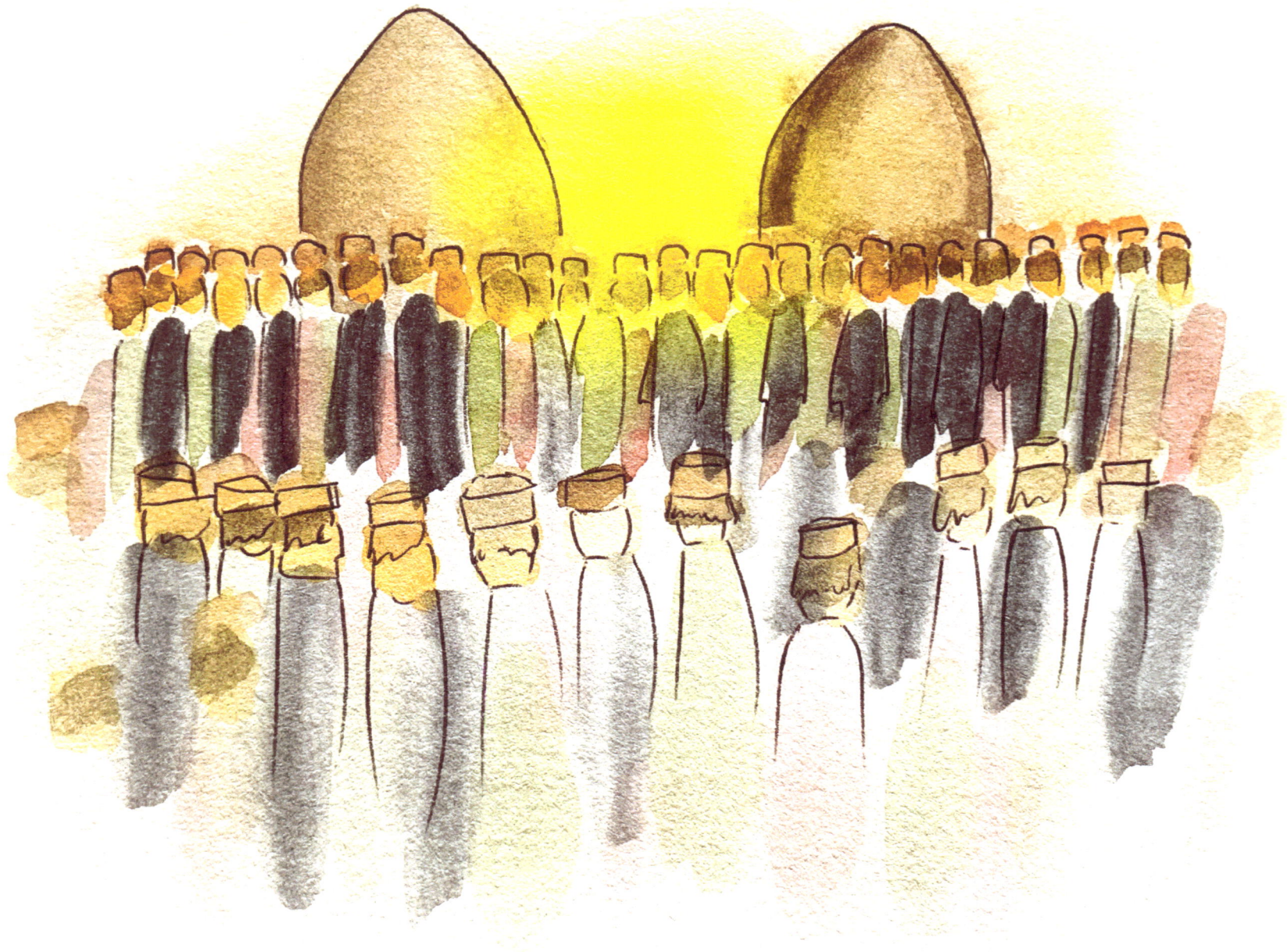

"Had you believed, O wayward generation,"
While new soldiers prepared for that wicked intention.

"Every one of you would have followed [...] this youth."
A young boy who comprehended the Eternal Truth.

"And willingly sacrifice yourself in My path."
Yet they chose not to. Alas. Alas.

"The day will come when you will have recognised Me."
Shining bright like the sun which we all can see.

"That Day I shall have ceased to be with you."
It breaks many a heart knowing this to be true.

Rifles now ready,
finger placed on the trigger,
with each row of bullets
the smoke grew thicker.

"Please stop!"
begged Alí, but it was too late.
The Báb and Anís
had accepted their fate.

Whirled up dust would not clear
for the rest of the day.
"What caused our hearts to lose its way?"

Ali wondered if ever
he would understand,
just Who that Man was
Who had walked our land.

He fell in a dream. A sweet voice he could hear.
The same voice that had called his heart come near.

It spoke to the seeker
all through the night:
"I am the Primal Point,
I am God's Light.

Assurance, all good
is in store for thee.
It is for whosoever
recognizes Me."*

Ali woke up at dawn.
"Dear mother let's pray.
I now understand, it is a new Day!

The Siyyid I saw is the Promised One.
The One, Holy Books
had foretold would come."

Ali's heart was at peace for what he had seen,
if not for God's will, would never have been.

This young boy had witnessed
the Báb meeting His fate.
Yet, this Faith would continue...

For the Báb was the Gate.

Dear children,

Wow. What a story. I pray you got some more insights into the Martyrdom of the Báb and find many opportunities to talk about this day and learn from it.

Did you know that there is a book called "The Dawn Breakers" which gives much more details of this historic day? I am sure you will come across it many times in your life.

Now it is your turn.

The Bahá'í faith might still be young, however in just over two-hundred years we are blessed to have many stories of people who have shown great courage, heroism, sacrifice and more.

With the help of someone you love, be a seeker of knowledge and find at least one story of a Bahá'í who has shown outstanding qualities such as sacrifice, kindliness, courage, servitude etc. Look around, you might already know one! But if not, I'm sure your mom, dad, older sibling, a member of your community or someone else you love and trust would be able to tell you many stories of one of the heroes of the Faith. So you could also ask them to share those with you.

Draw a picture, write a word, a sentence or a paragraph of what your heart felt inspired to after hearing the story.

If you like and are allowed to, I would love to see what you came up with. Tag me on Instagram @fresh_breeze_creations with your creation and/or with a picture while reading this book. You may also wish to memorize the final words of His holiness the Báb when He addressed the multitude before His martyrdom.

Much love and prayers coming your way, wherever you may be.

- Helen

Historical Context

The Báb means "The Gate". A befitting title for the One who prepared the way for the coming of Bahá'u'lláh, the supreme Manifestation of God who was soon to follow.

The Báb's given name was Siyyid 'Alí-Muhammad. He was born in 1819 in the city of Shíráz, South of Iran. He was primarily raised by His maternal uncle, as His father passed away in His early childhood.

There are many accounts of the Báb as a young child, which tell of His extraordinary, innate and indeed heavenly attributes. The Báb was only 25 years old, when He declared His mission on the evening of 22nd May 1844 to Mullá Hussayn, the first of His followers.

In a span of only six years the Bábi Faith spread rapidly throughout Iran. At this point in time, not only the people in Iran, but in fact many religious people around the world, were awaiting the coming of "the Promised One." As the Báb's claim challenged many longstanding traditions within the Muslim community, the government and clergy turned against the Báb, imprisoned Him for the last three years of His Ministry and finally gave the order which led to His martyrdom.

References

* Selection of the Writings of the Báb. Bahá'í World Centre, 1982 lightweight edition. P.217

Note:

1. The last image of the gate was created by Priscilla Senoga.

2. Ali is a fictional character. However, the historical events he observes are accurate.

To learn more about the Báb, His life and His teachings please visit https://www.bahai.org/the-bab

To learn more about the events surrounding the Martyrdom of the Báb please visit www.bahai.org/fr/the-bab/articles-resources/execution-the-bab

To watch the feature film "Dawn of the Light" commissioned by the Universal House of Justice in celebration of the Bicentenary of the Birth of the Báb please visit https://bicentenary.bahai.org/the-bab/

FRESH BREEZE
CREATIONS

www.ingramcontent.com/pod-product-compliance
Lightning Source LLC
Chambersburg PA
CBHW040712150426

42811CB00061B/1843